TABLE OF CONTE

True Colors

Words and Music by BILLY STEINBERG
and TOM KELLY

Yesterday

Words and Music by JOHN LENNON and PAUL McCARTNEY

Happy Together

Words and Music by GARRY BONNER and ALAN GORDON

We Are The World

Words and Music by LIONEL RICHIE and
MICHAEL JACKSON

Imagine

Words and Music by JOHN LENNON

Bad Day

Words and Music by
DANIEL POWTER

08

You Raise Me Up

Words and Music by BRENDAN
GRAHAM and ROLF LOVLAND

Fallin'

Words and Music by
ALICIA KEYS

11

A Hard Day's Night

Words and Music by JOHN LENNON
and PAUL McCARTNEY

Here Comes The Sun

Words and Music by
GEORGE HARRISON

Eye Of The Tiger

Words and Music by FRANK
SULLIVAN and JIM PETERIK

15

Happy

Words and Music by PHARRELL
WILLIAMS

Hallelujah

Words and Music by
LEONARD COHEN

Cups (When I'm Gone)

Words and Music by A.P. CARTER,LUISA GERSTEIN
and HELOISE TUNSTALL-BEHRENS

My Heart Will Go On
(Love Theme From Titanic)

Music by JAMES HORNER
Lyric by WILL JENNINGS

Roar

Words and Music by KATY PERRY, MAX MARTIN, DR.
LUKE, BONNIE McKEE and HENRY WALTER

Stay

Words and Music by MIKKY EKKO and JUSTIN PARKER

D.S. al Fine

Stay With Me

Words and Music by SAM SMITH, JAMES NAPIER, WILLIAM
EDWARD PHILLIPS, TOM PETTY and JEFF LYNNE

All Of Me

Words and Music by JOHN STEPHENS and
TOBY GAD

25

Rolling In The Deep

Words and Music by ADELE ADKINS and PAUL EPWORTH

Love Story

Words and Music by TAYLOR SWIFT

D.S al Coda

29

Viva La Vida

Words and Music by GUY BERRYMAN,JON BUCKLAND,
WILL CHAMPION and CHRIS MARTIN

Thinking Out Loud

Words and Music by ED SHEERAN
and AMY WADGE

33

Shake It Off

Words and Music by TAYLOR SWIFT, MAX
MARTIN and SHELLBACK

Firework

Words and Music by KATY PERRY,MIKKEL ERIKSEN, TOR
ERIK HERMANSEN,ESTHER DEAN and SANDY WILHELM

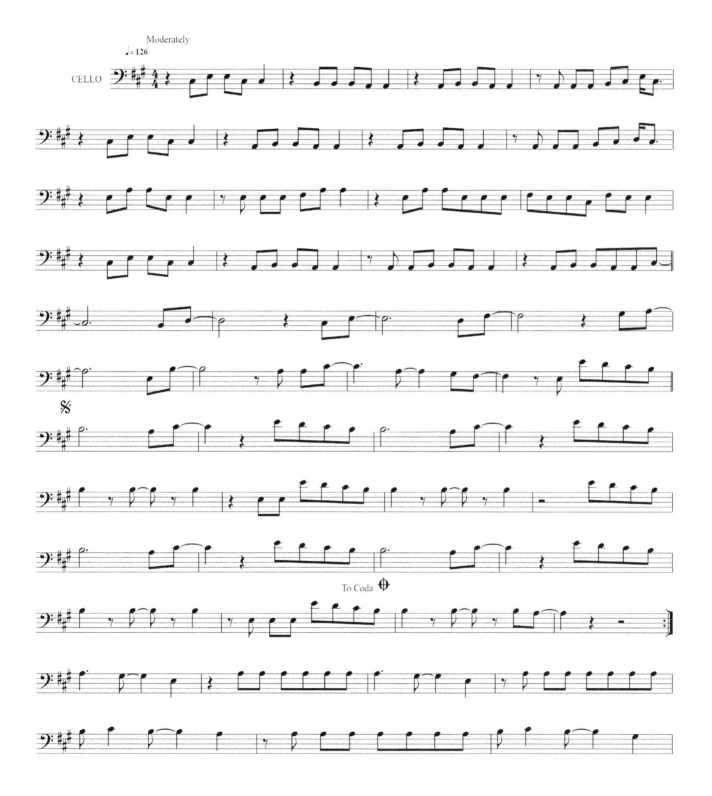

D.S. al Coda

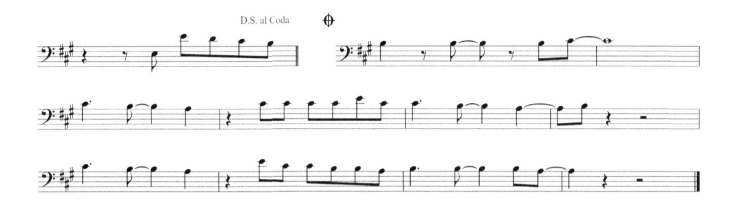

Secrets

Words and Music by
RYAN TEDDER

Brave

Words and Music by SARA
BAREILLES and JACK ANTONOFF

D.S. al Coda

A Thousand Years

Words and Music by DAVID HODGES
and CHRISTINA PERRI

Teenage Dream

Words and Music by KATY PERRY,BONNIE
McKEE, LUKASZ GOTTWALD,MAX
MARTIN and BENJAMIN LEVIN

Bad Romance

Words and Music by STEFANI
GERMANOTTA and NADIR KHAYAT

No One

Words and Music by ALICIA
KEYS,KERRY BROTHERS, JR. and
GEORGE HARRY

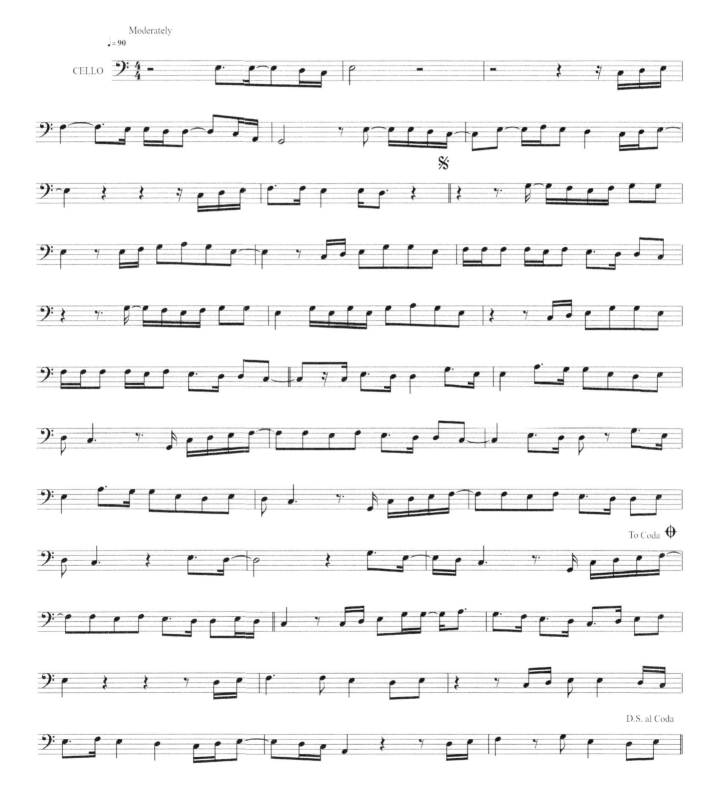

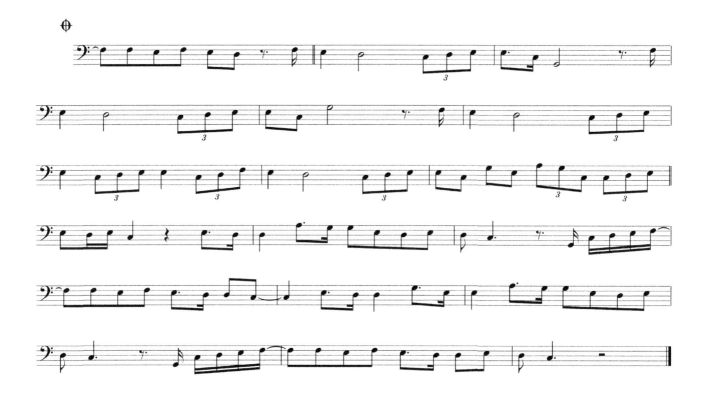

With Or Without You

Words and Music byU2

Somebody To Love

Words and Music by
FREDDIE MERCURY

Sweet Dreams
(Are Made Of This)

Words and Music by ANNIE LENNOX
and DAVID STEWART

Time In A Bottle

Words and Music by
JIM CROCE

Down Under

Words and Music by COLIN
HAY and RON STRYKERT

I Still Haven't Found What I'm Looking For

Words and Music by U2

Stairway To Heaven

Words and Music by JIMMY PAGE
and ROBERT PLANT

Shallow (from A Star Is Born)

Words and Music by STEFANI
GERMANOTTA,MARK RONSON, ANDREW
WYATT and ANTHONY ROSSOMANDO

Photograph

Words and Music by ED SHEERAN, JOHNNY McDAID,
MARTIN PETER HARRINGTON and TOM LEONARD

Perfect

Words and Music by SARA BAREILLES and
JACK ANTONOFF

Believer

Words and Music by DAN REYNOLDS, WAYNE SERMON, BEN
McKEE, DANIEL PLATZMAN, JUSTIN TRANTOR, MATTIAS
LARSSON and ROBIN FREDRICKSSON

No Tears Left To Cry

Words and Music by ARIANA GRANDE,SAVAN
KOTECHA, MAX MARTIN and ILYA

Dance Monkey

Words and Music byTONI WATSON

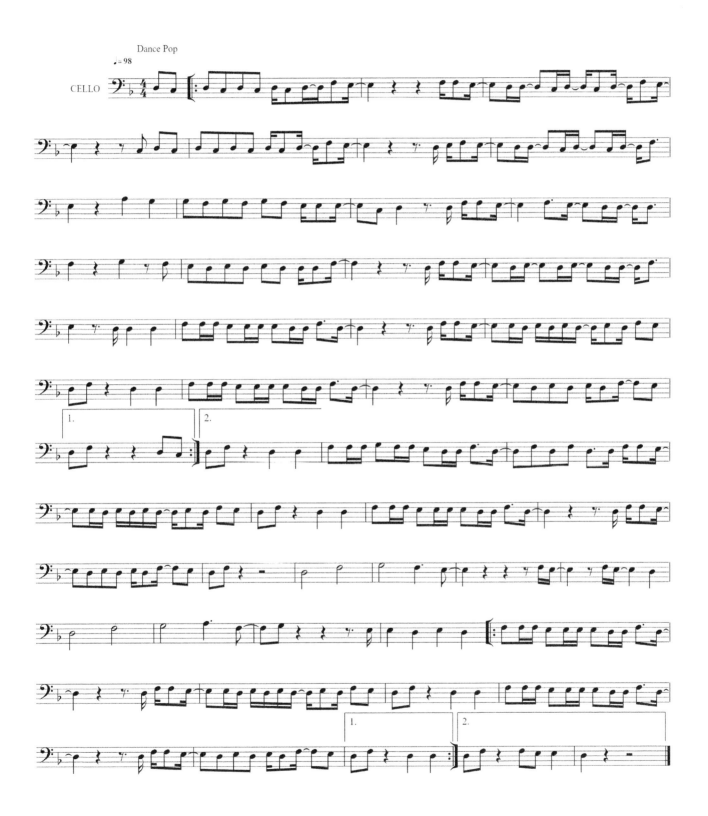

Song From A Secret Garden

By ROLF LOVLAND

Mamma Mia

Words & Music by Benny Andersson, Stig
Anderson & Björn Ulvaeus

Skyfall

Words and Music by ADELE ADKINS
and PAUL EPWORTH

Love Me Tender

Words and Music by ELVIS
PRESLEY and VERA MATSON

Printed in Great Britain
by Amazon

24767100R00040